Follow Me to the Staircase

Your Journey to Finding the Presence of God in Your Life

By

Dr Timothy Weir

Follow Me to the Staircase: Your Journey to Finding the Presence of God in Your Life
Author: Dr Timothy Weir
Copyright © 2024 by Dr. Timothy Weir
All rights reserved. No part of this book may be reproduced or transmitted in any form or by any means, electronic or mechanical, including photocopying, recording, or by any information storage and retrieval system without the written permission of the publisher, except for brief passages of text excerpted for use in media reviews.
Publisher: Self

All scripture quotations, unless otherwise noted, taken from the NLT, Holy Bible, New Living Translation Copyright (C) 1996, 2004, 2015 by Tyndale House Foundation. All rights reserved.

INTRODUCTION

I'm so glad you have this little book. This book was written from one of the Holy Spirit "Nudges" to me. He began to speak to me about it, and of course, I fought it. He speaks in a "still, small voice", but man can He get LOUD! He won!

This started from a lifetime of watching the Holy Spirit move. I realized that He flowed in churches when He was allowed to. But I also realized that He flowed in barbershops, ice cream parlors, restaurants and yes, even chiropractic offices. You see, everything is nothing if He is not allowed to "run the show". This wasn't a new thing for the 21st Century. I want to introduce you to my friend, Moses.

You see, God chose Moses to fix a problem. He had to get millions of people out of Egypt. It wasn't his fault that they were there, but God chose him. Here's what God didn't tell him before he did his first little miracle before Pharoah…these people were the biggest batch of grumbling and complaining people on the face of the earth. If you took them to the finest restaurant in the world, they would complain that the soup was not the right temperature, the steak had 22% too much gristle and using a non-foaming soap in the restrooms was just not up to par…at least…not their par.

As they have been in the Wilderness for years, finally God says… "I have had enough." He tells Moses, "Take this group of people to the promised land and get them settled. In Exodus 33:3, God tells Moses, I am going to send an angel with you to lead them, but I am not going *"You are a stubborn and rebellious people. If I were to travel with you for even a moment, I would destroy you."* Seriously! God tells them. You go, but I am not going because I might just kill all of you!

Moses is stuck. He would like to stay with God right there and let the crowd leave, but Moses calls for a meeting with God at the Tabernacle. They met. Let's look at it together. Exodus 33

13 If it is true that you look favorably on me, let me know your ways so I may understand you more fully and continue to enjoy your favor. And remember that this nation is your very own people."
14 The LORD replied, "I will personally go with you, Moses, and I will give you rest – everything will be fine for you."
15 Then Moses said, If you don't personally go with us, don't make us leave this place."
Man, how much less trouble we would get into if we just recognized this…if God isn't moving

with us...don't move! Without His presence, we get lost and in trouble!

16 How will anyone know that you look favorably on me – on me and on your people – if you don't go with us? For your presence among us sets your people and me apart from all other people on the earth."

Isn't that interesting? "Your presence among us sets your people and me apart from all other people on the earth." There are hundreds of religions throughout the world. They all teach great things. Most of them churn out wonderful neighbors, great families. There are Christian churches in your city that love Jesus. They feed the poor, they even have Sunday School. They teach how to live great lives...but there is no power. The Word of God says that He confirms His Word with signs, wonders and miracles. I want us to discover why we don't see it much in the church today.

17 "The LORD replied to Moses, "I will indeed do what you have asked, for I look favorably on you, and I know you by name."
18 Moses responded, "Then show me your glorious presence."

This book is a quest...a journey. I am looking for the gateway into the area where we can see God's glorious presence.

Everything is nothing if He is not allowed to "run the show".

CHAPTER ONE

I am here to help you find a way. A journey to discover the presence of the Spirit of God. To do that, I need to share a part of my journey. We have an exciting road ahead of us in the pages that follow. I want you to understand that you are a vessel that God wants to use to change your world and the world around you. The journey can't be bumpy and with all kinds of curves in the road…

I remember as a little boy, sitting in front of our black and white television set. I watched a man sitting in a folding chair on a stage, with people walking up to him. He would lay his hands on them, and I watched as people would stand up straighter or even get up from a wheelchair. I was glued to that television set watching him lay his hands on the young child who stuttered and immediately began to speak with normal diction. I saw a mother or father carrying their child up who had not walked since birth. It was simple. He would talk to them and then place his hands on their head and they would begin to stretch and move parts that they had never moved and by the end, that little one was walking or running. He often said, "Jesus is standing right beside me, and He is telling me to lay hands on you as a point of contact for Him to touch you." Miracle after miracle. It didn't matter if this person had never been to the inside of a church or they had never missed a church service, Jesus touched people. Something was imparted to me as I watched those miracles happen. I wanted to know that healing presence of Jesus…to feel Him standing next to me. God had placed in my heart the desire for more of Him.

It was years later, when I discovered that my father, who was in a wheelchair with M.S., had gotten out of a wheelchair as this man of God touched him. Years before, the doctors had given up on my father, giving him just a short time to live. My parents refused to accept this death sentence. They heard about the miracles that were happening under the Oral Roberts tent meetings, and they made the journey. He got out of the wheelchair and lived another 35 years. It was part of the journey, that whether they knew it or not, had started for me.

As I continued to walk with God, I had the unquenchable thirst to listen to and watch others who knew about this healing presence. I was mesmerized by the ministry of Kathryn Kuhlman. I would sit there for hours and watch her in her crusades at the Carnegie Auditorium in Pittsburg or at the Shrine Auditorium in California via videos. She would listen to the still, small voice of the Holy Spirit, and in faith or those words she heard, she reacted, and God moved. I remember her telling the audience that there was someone that had come who had been diagnosed with an incurable blood disease or a brain tumor and that Jesus was there to touch them. Sometimes you would hear a loud gasp or someone shouting way up in the audience. I heard her say, "Dear Sweet Jesus". She would ask, "Has something happened up there? Come up here, tell us what has happened." Here was this woman, simply being obedient to that still, small voice, fulfilling the great commission. She was laying hands on the sick, casting out demons. And watching those demons and diseases succumb to the sweet name of Jesus. Again, miracle after miracle.

Although I never went to her meetings or saw her in person, I felt like I knew her. In fact, my wife called her my "other wife"....I spent so much time watching her videos and listening. I was intrigued by her ability to hear the voice of God.

At this time, I had never heard of the Baptism of the Holy Spirit. I was raised in the church where you gave your heart to Jesus, and you got everything you were going to get right then. But I knew that there was more. I knew that there was a place we could go....to gain entrance into the very presence of God where we could believe and ask, and He would touch us. My hunger grew with greater intensity. I didn't know that I was myself on a journey of my own…I just knew there was something that they had…that I wanted.

Something was imparted to me as I watched those miracles happen. I wanted to know that healing presence of Jesus…to feel Him standing next to me.

CHAPTER TWO

When I was 5 years old, I played the piano for the Camp meetings for the Church of God 7th Day. I had a wonderful childhood in that church. I was blessed to have had pastors who recognized my gifts and helped to point me in the right direction. My first pastors were Vernon and Mary Patchen in our little church in New Auburn, Wisconsin. They were both incredibly talented in music. Vernon was an amazing piano player. He could "tickle the ivories" like nobody I knew. His wife Mary played the Hammond organ. Wow. Together, they were so matched. I was around 4-5 years old, and after the service, I would ask Mary if I could play some songs on her Hammond. She was always so willing to let me do that, and it was the highlight of my week. They left our church and went to serve at Spring Vale Academy, where later I would go as a student. Although Vernon has gone to be with the Lord, Mary is there, still serving. A bit later, we had new pastors come. Delvin and Wilma O'Banion. Wilma was the one who recognized my vocal skills and aimed me further in that direction. It was during this time that I spent time learning the scriptures. My mother and father scrimped, saved, and put me in a Christian Elementary School, where I learned more about living a Godly life. I learned more of my music there, but I also learned scripture. It is so important to invest in the lives of your children as far as their education. I know it is a lot...but we are talking about their eternal future.

 I remember when I was 5 years old, I played the piano for the Camp meetings for the General Conference Conventions for the entire country. I couldn't read a lick of music, but I could sit at a piano and play songs that I had just heard. By the time I was in high school, I toured the United States and Canada with the Kuryluk Family Singers. I would play and sing with them. We would put on services for people in the churches around the country. I then attended the church boarding school in Michigan. I was deeply involved in the music, playing for most of the church services and again touring the states representing the school in a music team.

Once I graduated, I thought God was wanting me to do more with my musical talents. I discovered that I could capture my singing and playing in a recording studio. So, in 1976, my new bride and I drove to Nashville, Tenn, and recorded my gospel album at Rockland Road Studios. I met the owners of the studio, the Oakridge Boys Quartet. It was the week that they switched from "Gospel music" to "Country". I recorded my album and even introduced a song I had just written, "Give Us Peace," that became the cover song. With that album, Rose and I toured the country from shore to shore. We would put on "concerts" at various churches. We met a lot of incredible people. One of those churches was in Sacramento, California. I was told years later that a young man at that church bought my album and played it over and over. I was told that he became deathly ill and passed away. His one request was that they play my album at his funeral. I sang, played the piano, met thousands of people who loved my songs, but in that, I knew that there was more. I knew that there was a presence of God that I still was not able to touch. I knew that there was more to this than a concert.

CHAPTER THREE

Remember my dad? He had been healed but was also helped greatly with chiropractic care. Remember, I knew Jesus as savior, and I knew that He could heal, but I was not sure how all the healing fit into church. I knew He had called me as a "healer", but I thought for sure it was as a chiropractor. I just felt like it was the "foot in the door". I studied and in 1981, graduated from Palmer College of Chiropractic in Davenport, Iowa. I studied the body and how it worked…not just the spine. We were required to study the various systems and how they worked. Finally, it was time for the caps and gowns. But right before graduation, I received a call from one of the pastors at Westside Assembly in Davenport, Iowa. It was a huge Assemblies of God church. You know…the "Holy Rollers". They had heard my album and asked me if I would come and sing for this huge church. They would have a service once a year, honoring the Palmer College of Chiropractic graduates, and I seemed to fit right into that service. I was to sing right before the pastor, Tommy Barnett preached. I responded to their phone call inviting me to sing with "Of Course." In this service, I was introduced to worship. Singing and praising Jesus like he was standing in front of you. I saw people raise their hands in the service. It was incredible. Remember, I was used to singing from a hymnal…not from words "off the wall" It was surreal. I witnessed an altar call with dozens of people coming forward to turn their hearts over to Jesus. It was my first encounter with the Assemblies of God Church…but not my last.

CHAPTER FOUR

I left Davenport, Iowa and started my chiropractic career. It was at this time, that I had a realization, I was born in Wisconsin, but I was a "southerner" in heart." I worked hard to build my practice. We were still members of the Church of God 7th Day and attended a church in N.C. At the same time, the little church in Farmville, NC asked me to be their "part-time pastor". It was great; I could practice during the week and on the weekend, preach, and minister. It was during this time, that I was introduced to some crazy people. These dear friends introduced me to something new. People who believed in healing and the baptism of the Holy Spirit. I heard people like Kenneth Copeland, Jerry Seville, John Osteen. They opened a door for me...the Baptism of the Holy Spirit. I asked the Lord to Baptize me in the Holy Spirit, with the evidence of speaking in tongues and He did. My life changed forever.

It is amazing how the steps of a righteous man are ordered by the Lord. Even marrying my high school sweetheart, she had pieces to the puzzle of where God was taking me. She came from a family of amazing preachers. Probably the most famous one was the Methodist evangelist, Tommy Tyson. I had never heard of him, but he was known all over the world. It was

Tommy Tyson who was a part of the life of Oral Roberts and he ministered to Kenneth Copeland. At family reunions, I was able to spend some time with Tommy and glean a bit of his wisdom and his experience that would be a part of the picture of my life that God was putting together. Don't discount where you are right now. God has you there for a purpose. Your steps are being ordered by the Lord. Let your prayer be, "Lord, why am I here? What do you need me to learn and who do I need to touch for you?"

For the next 30 years, I was enrolled in school. Not a college or university, but in the school of the prophets. My teacher was the Holy Spirit. My textbook was the Bible. Acts 17:10-11 says, *"That very night the believers sent Paul and Silas to Berea. When they arrived there, they went to the Jewish synagogue. And the people of Berea were more open-minded than those in Thessalonica, and they listened eagerly to Paul's message. They searched the Scriptures day after day to see if Paul and Silas were teaching the truth."*

I had become a Berean. I gleaned what I could from the Word and added to that all the things I had learned on my journey to this point.

It was our pastor in Marshfield, Wisconsin, who opened our eyes to the Holy Spirit and His gifts. He was instrumental in helping us navigate from a legalistic background to the freedom of the Spirit. Not only was he a funny, incredible speaker, but he was also a worshipper and a worship leader. We learned so much about the music the opens the doors to the Heavenlies. (more about this later) We then moved to Raleigh, NC for a "job", but it was the Holy Spirit moving us to another "school".

We were well grounded in the Word from an incredible pastor, Robert Spradley. Rob and Diane had just moved to Raleigh to start a brand-new church, Raleigh Christian Community. He had served as Youth Pastor at Calvary Assembly in Orlando, Florida and he started the Jesus Movement in Florida. He mentored us well in the Word of God. We learned a lot from him. He was an incredible worship musician who loved God with all of his heart. He wrote one of my favorite worship songs, "I need you". Remember, I had been entrusted with some amazing gifts from the Holy Spirit. I would find myself "knowing" things that were happening in people's lives and their bodies. I sensed when there was cancer or disease in someone's body. I would lay my hands on people and people would walk away with no pain, or a large tumor gone. I would tell them about a decision they were getting ready to make, and how it would be a detrimental step in their lives. I learned this as the spiritual gift, the "word of knowledge". I think I drove poor Robert crazy. He was trying to run a church, and I was trying to figure out this Holy Spirit stuff.

I began to ask God for someone to teach me more about the stuff "behind the curtain" and into the Holy of Holies. One day, a man walked into my clinic, and he was God's answer for my missing pieces. Dr. Mark Chironna.

I talked to Pastor Chironna about my gifts and how I was kind of frustrated in what I was hearing and doing. I knew the Holy Spirit was speaking to me, but I did not know how to practically use these gifts. He understood completely.

Pastor Mark invited me to come to his church to minister to his church. I had never heard him speak or minister, but I went to minister to his body of believers. That night was an incredible step for me. I was free to speak and minister the Word of God and then allow the Holy Spirit to flow. People were touched, and so was I. As I was ministering during an altar time, Mark came up and began to flow in the gifts of the Spirit as well. I was praying for a lady to be healed of something. As I was praying for her, Mark came up and said to her, "You have a ring in your bedroom. It was given to you by an aunt a couple of years ago. That ring has a demonic curse on it. When you get home, I want you to throw that ring away. Don't give it away to someone else; throw it away." That lady was "slain in the Spirit" and stood up completely healed. I knew that I had gone from grade school, through high school and now I was in the college part of my "School of the Prophets".

For over 20 years, we served under his ministry. We watched him grow from where he was in ministry to a worldwide ministry. He was gracious with me, teaching me how to open up the gates to the heavens and then use the gifts that God had invested in me to minister to people. I grew in wisdom and my understanding of the Word and the gifts of the Holy Spirit. I was honored to have been able to watch and learn so much about the work of the Holy Spirit. God was blessing us as we blessed others. I found foundations in my gifts. I knew that when I spoke a word over someone's life, it was from God, and whether they acknowledged it or not, it was true. I knew that if I called out a disease or addiction, someone may have one of those, but too embarrassed to come up…but I knew beyond the shadow of a doubt that they were there in that building. I was recently in a ministry time during a service and the Holy Spirit began to speak. One of those words of knowledge was that there was someone in that room that God was delivering from a Cocaine addiction. Of course, no body stood up, jumping up and down screaming, "It's me...it's me!" But I know that person was there and God did set them free. They may possibly contact me and tell me their story, but even if they don't, I know God spoke.

I found that the healing gifts spilled over into my practice as well. People were touched by God as I treated them as their chiropractor. I was able to speak words from God to them. It was incredible.

I often went with him to different cities where he ministered at churches or conventions and watched him minister to people. All the time, I was listening to him and learning how to be God's hands to touch people. I remember flying to Long Island, New York as he was ministering at a large church there. Little did I know that he had been preparing the ground for me to join him that night to minister to that church. He told me, "I told everyone that you are going to be joining me tonight to help minister. I told them that you were Kathryn Kuhlman wearing pants." Wow. Once again, God moved.

Dr. Chironna and his family felt God's hand to move them to Orlando to start a church and ministry there. His television ministry had taken off, and he was on the road a lot of time at various places he was asked to come and minister.

He now oversees many pastors and churches and serves as Bishop Mark Chironna. By this time, my practice had taken off and it was impossible for us to go with them…although we flew down a couple of times per month to help them with their children's ministry…until 9-11. His mentoring and love helped me understand this incredible work of the Holy Spirit.

CHAPTER FIVE

It was at this time; we went through what I lovingly call a "wilderness experience." We went from church to church, trying to find a place to "fit in". You must understand the ministry and being the pastor. Their job is to protect the flock and having someone who had served at the level we had, we could not find a pastor that would allow us to come in and be a part of their congregations. When they slept at night, they would keep one eye open, watching us. They were afraid we were just wanting to come in and take over their ministry. We didn't want to serve or anything…we just wanted a place to rest. We felt like we were stuck in no man's land. We just stopped looking. We stopped going. We just waited to see what God was going to do. It was during this time that I studied. I looked at all the major religions and tried to figure out what they were trying to do for people. I looked at the Hindus, the Muslims, and even studied the Scientology religion. None of them could offer anything to fill the void that people in their hearts that only Jesus could satisfy.

The only thing that I knew, was from the age of 5, God had a plan and a purpose. I had the dream in my heart of music and somehow, I knew that I was a healer.

Remember Joseph? He had a dream. His dreams, although very symbolic, were dreams that told his future. He had no idea what they meant totally or how he would get there, but he held those dreams tightly to his heart. He shared those dreams with his brothers, and even though they turned on him and wanted to destroy him, God still had a future and a plan for him. Eventually, even through some tough times, he came out on the other side. It was those rough times that created who he became. It wasn't until his brothers out of desperation came to Egypt to buy grain that the dream finally, made total sense. All the hurts, traumas and pain were all worth it all and he was able to take those and become the salvation for his entire family.

Realize that although the road is hard…you're still here. The fact that you picked up this book and are reading it, is Gods hand on your life. It is your GPS turning on telling you… "you're on the right road….keep going until you see your next turn".

"Eventually, even through some tough times, he came out on the other side. It was those rough times that created who he became."

CHAPTER SIX

That next turn happened for us a couple of years ago when we met Pastor Chad Harvey and a group of renegade believers. Why renegade? When Covid hit the country, Raleigh First Assembly was the only church that stayed open and continued to worship and teach. He is one of my favorite teacher/preachers. He has an acute sensitivity to the voice of God. He doesn't hold back in teaching. Oh, I'm sure that he has gotten a lot of slack over the years for it, but He doesn't compromise the Word. He is funny. Some time ago, I was worried about inserting humor into my messages, and the Lord told me that if I could distract people and make them laugh, He could touch them and heal them. Chad Harvey has just the right mix of this!

He has an incredible call for men to be men and be lovers of God…lead their families and serve God. Salvation is far more than saying a little prayer…it is switching the Lordship in your life from you running the show to Jesus Christ being the Lord.

His mission statement for the church is "Cross Assembly" is a missions-sending base. We build up and send out Spirit-filled agents of local and global transformation." His purpose in teaching and preaching is to train the people in the congregation for the work of the ministry. He believes that you aren't just a church member, but you are on a mission from God to the world. They are a mission sending base to over 200 families who have left Raleigh for Global Missions. That is a testimony to the vision that God gave him.

For the past 3 years, we have found our home at Cross Assembly.

CHAPTER SEVEN

As we look at the lives of those who have gone before and those now who understand God of what it means to be called and anointed, you begin to realize the weight of that same calling. We have taken a relationship and turned it into something so far less than that...a "hobby". Most Christians want to blend into the world, and God is saying "don't be a part of the world...stand out." A lot of people attend church on Sunday, giving God 9am-noon, and then they retain control over the other 165 hours in the week. This relationship that God wants to have with you cost Him everything...His Son and He wants the same from you. He takes it rather seriously.

For you to understand how this works, you have to understand the fact that it boils down to God wanting to have a relationship with you. He absolutely loves spending time with you. Step number one in your relationship with God, is that God speaks to you. That is how it started since the beginning of the world.

It starts at the beginning of the book in the book of Genesis. Basically, God created this entire playground, birds, seas, grass, trees, the firmament with stars, and monkeys and then at the very end of creation, God added man in His

image to be the superintendent of this theme park. God was happy. The scripture tells us that God spent time with Adam and Eve, talking to them, walking with them, and sharing life with them. Talk about trying to "hear God speak". They heard God speak! There was nothing in the way at this point. They talked to Him, and He talked to them. Imagine walking around this creation with the creator and talking to Him. I want you to remember this time because we are going to come back to this. If you are over 55, you may remember the old hymn, written by Charles Miles in 1913, "In the Garden".
"I come to the garden alone,
While the dew is still on the roses,
And the voice I hear falling on my ear
The Son of God discloses.

Refrain:
And He walks with me, and He talks with me,
And He tells me I am His own;
And the joy we share as we tarry there,
None other has ever known.

He speaks, and the sound of His voice
Is so sweet the birds hush their singing,
And the melody that He gave to me
Within my heart is ringing.

And finally the 3rd Verse…
I'd stay in the garden with Him,

Though the night around me be falling,
But He bids me go; through the voice of woe
His voice to me is calling.

In 1913, Charles Miles had a glimpse of what it was like to talk to the creator. I know that was a long song, but you needed to hear it.

As we are well aware, Adam and Eve messed up big time. They blew it. He had the ultimate relationship with God. But he allowed his humanity to cause a stumble. And yet, God doesn't give up on man. Remember, His ultimate scenario is to have a relationship with man. From Genesis until Matthew 28, Jehovah is working on His plan. A plan of redemption. He paid the ultimate price, the life of His son, to pay for a debt that was accumulated and pitted against you. From the fall in Genesis, everyone who was born was now born into the wrong family. There was now a separation from God because of that fall…but God had a plan

CHAPTER EIGHT

The Old Testament is filled with points in history when God continued to speak to His people. Genesis 6 speaks of how far the world had gone wrong. Evil filled the world, and yet there were still people who believed that God had a plan. They listened and they heard God speak. As God is getting ready to shut down the entire theme park, God sees Noah. I love Genesis 6:9, *"This is the account of Noah and his family. Noah was a righteous man, the only blameless person living on earth at the time, and he walked in close fellowship with God."* Wow. Lord, help me to be like Noah. And God brings Noah into His plan. Imagine, the creator of the world shares the future of the world with this guy. Genesis 6:11, *"Now God saw that the earth had become corrupt and was filled with violence. God observed all this corruption in the world, for everyone on earth was corrupt. So God SAID TO NOAH, "Build an ark"*. I don't know about you, but I have a hard time writing this without hearing Bill Cosby saying… "NOAH, NOAH…Build me an Ark". I know, that is carbon dating for me.

Now, understand this…God is tired of people trampling all over his creation. So, God speaks again. Noah listens. You have to understand that the people of that time lived much longer than we do now. Many scholars claim he was

500 when he was told to build an ark. Those same scholars claim it took 20-50 years to build it. Talk about believing the word of the Lord. Can you imagine his neighbors? "We had a nice neighborhood until the kook in the cul-de-sac started to build this huge…I'm talking HUGE Boat in his back yard. He ruined the neighborhood. Edna, tell the man…he ruined out neighborhood." For 50 years he is telling people that the Lord told him it is going to rain and there is going to be a flood. That flood is going to wipe everything out. You better repent. So not only does poor Noah have to start a huge construction project, he also has to start a new ministry. "Repent or Drown Ministries International, LLC". He is trying to build this massive ship, get people to repent, keep his marriage together, raise children, oh, I forgot…and become a zoo keeper. So the next time you complain about God giving you a word to put an extra $50.00 in the collection plate, Noah doesn't want to hear it.

CHAPTER NINE

Further down the line, God speaks to a man whose name was Abram. He speaks to him too, and Abram hears him. You see, God has a plan and He is working the plan. He hasn't given up. He knows what needs to happen. So here is Abram, an old man, he is 99 years old by now. A man who loved God. He is married to his wife, Sarah. She is no spring chicken either. So God says to Abram, listen, I want you to have children. You thought Gods word to you was unbelievable, what was Abram thinking. Don't believe me, read it in Genesis 17.

1 "When Abram was ninety-nine years old, the Lord appeared to him and said, "I am El-Shaddai – 'God Almighty.' Serve me faithfully and live a blameless life.
2 I will make a covenant with you, by which I will guarantee to give you countless descendants.

3 At this, Abram fell face down on the ground. Then God said to him, 4 "This is my covenant with you: I will make you the father of a multitude of nations!
5 What's more, I am changing your name. It will no longer be Abram. Instead, you will be called Abraham, for you will be the father of many nations. 6 I will make you extremely fruitful. Your descendants will become many nations, and kings will be among them!"

Now, the name change is the kicker. God could have just said, you are going to be a father, but not just a father, the father of many nations. No, that would have been too easy. God decides to change his name from Abram to Abraham. Cool name, except it means "Father of many nations." Here is the problem. The post office is going to get his name change form. The Social Security office is getting his name change form. The mailbox goes from Abram to Abraham. He has to change all of his business cards…now they all say ABRAHAM: FATHER OF MANY NATIONS. Do you get it? Every time he introduces himself, he is saying, "I'm the Father of Many Nations". Do you know how much faith it took to say that? Do you now understand why Romans 4:17 says that *"Abraham called things that were not, as though they G."* In other words, there were no outward signs of anything that was going to happen. In fact, all the outward "facts" pointed in the opposite direction. But Abraham, looked at his old body, and the body of his old wife, and decided to believe God's Word to him and he continued to announce, "I am the father of many nations".

Please do me a favor and read all of Genesis, except, read it with this in mind…God is still talking to men!

In fact, read the entire Old Testament again. Read it and look for all the people that God called and He spoke to them. Moses, Aaron, Caleb, and Joshua, and then look at Samuel.

CHAPTER TEN

I love this story. It is the combination of lives to fulfill a plan and a purpose. Eli is the priest in the Tabernacle. He is God's man of the hour, and yet, his boys dishonor God and it. There is "sin in the camp," and because of this, God isn't speaking. Did you hear that? Because sin was present, God wasn't. But God had a plan. God's plan was to bring someone back into His house who had a heart after Him and could hear His voice.

Enter Hannah. This lady was barren. She could not conceive. She and her man tried but to no avail. But Hannah didn't give up. She knew the stories. She had heard that God still speaks to people and God has a plan. So, she had enough faith to believe that if she were to ask, God would give her a son. She went to the Tabernacle to pray….to speak to God and beg Him for a son. In fact, she was so enthralled in prayer that her lips moved, but words didn't come out. We are going to talk more about this later. Old Eli thought she was drunk…but when she poured out her heart to him, as the priest, He spoke the word of the Lord and said in I Samuel 1:17, *"…Eli said go in peace. May the God of Israel grant the request you have asked of Him"*….and 9 months later…the word of the Lord came to pass. She promised the Lord when he was born that she would present him to serve Him. So, when he was 3-5 years old, Hannah took little Samuel to live in the Tabernacle to live with Eli. There aren't too many of us who wouldn't consider reneging on this promise we made. Imagine, taking this little guy who you have fallen in love with and leaving him at the Tabernacle with an old man.

Of interest in this story is that Eli, the priest, had raised sons who were to carry on the lineage of the priesthood, and yet Eli did not teach them how to hear God. They didn't listen to the voice of God but listened to the voice of money, sex, and power. In I Samuel 2:27, the account is listed where a "man of God" came to Eli and laid him out. His children would die at an early age, and he would not see his offspring carry on the ministry of the priesthood. Like Adam…he blew it. But God still had a plan. He knew. None of this was a surprise to Him. He already had His secret agent in place, a little boy named Samuel. A little boy who had heard his momma tell the story a thousand times of how she spoke to God, and God HEARD her and that Samuel had a call on his life. And while "in those days messages from the Lord were very rare and visions were quite uncommon…. SUDDENLY, God called out SAMUEL". God had a plan.

That plan continued through David and Solomon, and we see God performing creative miracles through Elisha and Elijah. We see the faith of the Shunamite woman who heard the word of the Lord and believed the man of God and would not waiver. Suddenly, God is speaking again because He had again found people who would believe Him and listen. Isaiah, Jeremiah, Ezekiel, Daniel, Hosea, Joel, Amos, Obadiah, Nahum, Habakkuk, Zephaniah, Zechariah, and Malachi all heard the voice…the still, small voice and believed it and spoke the Word given. They spoke even when there was no physical presence….but a voice. They shared the "thus saith the Lord", even when it didn't make sense. They were obedient.

CHAPTER ELEVEN

Step number one is to understand that God is still speaking. He speaks in a still small voice. You know it. You hear it. You may not recognize it or be able to hear it because of the noise of life. You see, from Genesis until Matthew 28, it was part one of the plan. Part two is when these people who trust in their God and their lives are completely changed through the death, burial, and resurrection of Jesus Christ, then they are no longer just a human on earth; they are now the Body of Christ on earth to continue to do what He started. The redemption of the world.

God speaks. We often don't hear it because of all of the other noise in our lives. Radio, television, Podcasts, News, cellphones….Noise! Want to hear God a little more? Turn down the other noise!

CHAPTER TWELVE

Genesis 28 gives the account of Jacob, the son of Isaac. Here is a guy who lived in a conflict with his brother Esau. So, Isaac calls for Jacob to come to him so he can bless him. He basically passed on the blessing of Abraham and sent him away to live with his uncle Laban and find a good wife. Remember, American Airlines was not around so he traveled a good distance by camel. He is tired, so the entire caravan stops for the night, and Jacob falls into a deep sleep, in that deep sleep, God speaks to him in a dream. Job 33:18 says, *"He speaks in dreams, in visions of the night when deep sleep falls on people as they lie in their beds. He whispers in their ears."* In the middle of the night, God gave him a vision.

Look at what we see starting in Genesis 28:12... *"As he slept, he dreamed of a stairway that reached from the earth up to heaven. And he saw the angels of God going up and down the stairway. At the top of the stairway stood the Lord, and He said 'I am the Lord, the God of your grandfather Abraham and the God of your father Isaac. The ground you are lying on belongs to you. I am giving it to you and your descendants."* When we skip down to verse 16, it says *"Then Jacob awoke from his sleep and said, 'Surely the Lord is in this place, and I wasn't even aware of it!' but he was also afraid and said 'What an awesome place this is! It is not other than the house of God,* **THE VERY GATEWAY TO HEAVEN'"**

Then look at verse 18… *"The next morning Jacob got up very early."* By the way, this is one of my first lessons from Robert Spradley; he called it "prime time." Getting up early in the morning and spending time in prayer and study. It started way back over 40 years ago, and I still get up early to seek the presence of God. I must confess…I am not an "early morning kind of guy." It takes me a while to wake up. I am very quiet in the early morning. I don't jump out of bed with a spring in my step and song on my lips. Some early versions of the Bible call this "grumpy". For the first 20 years of my marriage, Rose thought I was mad at her. She finally realized that I wasn't mad…I just wasn't awake. But this early morning time with God has helped form a little tabernacle where we meet every morning.

So, he continues in verse 18… *"He took the stone he had rested his head against, and he set it upright as a memorial pillar. Then he poured olive oil over it."* In verse 19 the word says *"He named that place Bethel (which means 'house of God')"*

There is an arena we enter when suddenly the Heavens open and we have access to the very presence of God. The place where all doubt and fear leave, and we are faced with endless possibilities. It is the place of the miraculous and the incredible. It is the storehouse of miracles and the creative. It is the place where resources are unlimited, and power is endless. It is the place where sin is exterminated, and sickness cannot exist. Oh, if we can find the entrance to that place. It is a sacred place.

CHAPTER THIRTEEN

Let's go forward now to the incredible ministry of the prophet Elijah. This guy walked and talked with God. He heard the voice of God and knew that He was now the voice of God on the earth. He spoke the word from God and kings listened, and history was changed. Sometimes we forget about these incredible men of God and the price they paid.

We could spend days talking just about Elijah and his ministry. That is a topic for later discussion. I want to simply take you to his final day on earth. Get ready…put on your seatbelt. Go with me to 2 Kings 2:1. *"When the Lord was about to take Elijah up to heaven."* HOLD THE PRESS. I didn't think anybody could go to heaven. But here God is about to take Elijah UP to heaven. How could he get there? It seems he would need stairs or an elevator to get him there. Sorry…keep reading… *"When the Lord was about to take Elijah up to heaven in a whirlwind, Elijah and Elisha were traveling from Gilgal. And Elijah said to Elisha, "stay here, for the Lord has told me to go to BETHEL. Elijah said to Elisha, "Stay here; the LORD has sent me to Bethel." But Elisha said, "As surely as the LORD lives and as you live, I will not leave you."* So they went down to Bethel.
3 The company of the prophets at Bethel came out to Elisha and asked, "Do you know that the LORD is

going to take your master from you today?" "Yes, I know," Elisha replied, *"so be quiet."* Here is a group of prophets of the Lord who lived where? In Bethel. If you wanted to be around the presence of God, what better place could you live? They all heard the word of the Lord. Oh my, God is still speaking. Then Elisha says...I KNOW.

Many times, God will use you to speak a confirming word to someone. They already know what you are going to tell them, but sometimes it is important to hear it so that you know you are heading in the right direction or making the right decision.

I was at a point where I was trying to decide what God wanted me to do in my life. It was rather stressful. So stressful in fact, that my heart began skipping beats and acting rather strangely. I went to a cardiologist, and he wanted me to wear a heart monitor. I would have to wear it 24 hours a day for 3 days. I had forgotten that Marilyn Hickey was coming to town and we had planned to go. At the end of the service, she started to minister to people. Hundreds of people got in a line to go past her. For 90% of the people she simply laid her hands on them. When I got to her, she grabbed my hands and gave me a Word from a scripture that completely answered my questions. I did not "fall under the power" or anything like that, but I knew that God had met me that night. Two days after these meeting, I had my visit with the cardiologist. They took off the monitor, and told me they were going to download it and the cardiologist would read it and then meet me. I sat for about an hour waiting, and finally he came in. He was acting kind of strange. He said, "what happened two nights ago about 9:15"? I said "why"? Well at that moment, it is almost like a bolt of lightning hit the monitor and it is burned up". He told me that they wanted to redo another test. I said, "NOT ME". I walked out, never had another symptom…. but I knew God's plan! That is the power of the confirmatory word of knowledge!

These two guys continue on a journey. Elijah hears God and takes them to Jerico and then the Jordan river. As what happened in Bethel and in Jerico, more prophets came and confirmed what God was about to do. Look at this account starting in verse 6. *"Then Elijah said to him, "Stay here; the LORD has sent me to the Jordan." And he replied, "As surely as the LORD lives and as you live, I will not leave you." So, the two of them walked on. 7 Fifty men from the company of the prophets went and stood at a distance, facing the place where Elijah and Elisha had stopped at the Jordan.*

8 Elijah took his cloak, rolled it up and struck the water with it. The water divided to the right and left, and the two crossed over on dry ground." **Sounds familiar, right? Are you singing that little children's song... "How did Moses cross the Red Sea"? I am. Moses did the same thing.** *9 When they had crossed, Elijah said to Elisha, "Tell me, what can I do for you before I am taken from you?" "Let me inherit a double portion of your spirit," Elisha replied.*
10 "You have asked a difficult thing," Elijah said, "yet if you see me when I am taken from you, it will be yours — otherwise, it will not."
11 As they were walking along and talking together, suddenly a chariot of fire and horses of fire appeared and separated the two of them, and Elijah went up to heaven in a whirlwind.
12 Elisha saw this and cried out, "My father! My father! The chariots and horsemen of Israel!" And Elisha saw him no more. Then he took hold of his garment and tore it in two.
13 Elisha then picked up Elijah's cloak that had fallen from him and went back and stood on the bank of the Jordan.
14 He took the cloak that had fallen from Elijah and struck the water with it. "Where now is the LORD, the God of Elijah?" he asked. When he struck the water, it divided to the right and to the left, and he crossed over." **Don't you know, he wanted to see if this thing would work. It was an easy way to**

see if he got the "double portion" of the anointing. It worked!

15 "The company of the prophets from Jericho, who were watching, said, "The spirit of Elijah is resting on Elisha." And they went to meet him and bowed to the ground before him."

You are going to find something about this anointing of the Holy Spirit. It is a substance. You see, as Elijah wore this cloak year after year, it soaked up the presence of God. Every time Elijah heard God speak, a little anointing rubbed off on the cloak. When he touched the degenerated hip and God healed it, a part of that anointing was transferred into those threads. When he spoke before the people of God, proclaiming the Word, part of that anointing was saturating that cloak.

I remember ministering years ago at a Women's Aglow meeting, and the Spirit of God began to move. I prayed for over 100 people that night with prophetic words and laying hands on the sick. God moved in such an incredible fashion. Towards the end of the service, I was getting warm, so I took off my suit coat and threw it towards a lady to hold on to it, and as soon as it hit her, she fell down under the power of God. The Holy Spirit healed her body with just my suit coat. Well, Dr. Weir, that is just plain WEIRD. It may have happened to Elijah, but that was the Old Testament. Ok Karen, look at Acts 19:12.

Paul has been preaching and ministering, and in verse 12, it says, *"When handkerchiefs or aprons that had merely touched his skin were placed on sick people, they were healed of their diseases, and evil spirits were expelled."* This power was so powerful it was able to be soaked up by a piece of clothing, and it was transferable from one man to another.

Before we leave 2 Kings, I want to share something with you. Elijah is taken up in a whirlwind. He encounters the Holy Spirit here at the Jordan river. May I take you to this same spot hundreds of years later, when a young man from Nazareth was beginning His ministry, He went to the Jordan river to be baptized. In Matthew 3:16, the writer pens these words *"After his baptism, as Jesus came up out of the water, the heavens were opened, and he saw the Spirit of God descending like a dove and settling on him."* He had a supernatural encounter with the Holy Spirit. From that point on, He walked in a new anointing…a fresh infilling of the presence of God. Don't you wish we could have that today?

CHAPTER FOURTEEN

Acts 2 tells us about another Bethel…another staircase.

1 "On the day of Pentecost all the believers were meeting together in one place. 2 Suddenly, there was a sound from heaven like the roaring of a mighty windstorm, and it filled the house where they were sitting. 3 Then, what looked like flames or tongues of fire appeared and settled on each of them."

Isn't it interesting that the Word of God uses the term that means "tongue" to describe the Holy Spirit resting on people?

4 "And everyone present was filled with the Holy Spirit and began speaking in other languages, or other tongues as the Holy Spirit gave them this ability." It is that same whirlwind that took Elijah UP that is now bringing down the presence of God to the world…and it hasn't stopped. Continue to read in Acts 2 because Peter gets up and begins to preach to the people who were there. The end result of that message starts in verse 37 *"Peter's words pierced their hearts, and they said to him and to the other apostles, "Brothers, what should we do?"*

38 Peter replied, "Each of you must repent of your sins and turn to God and be baptized in the name of Jesus Christ for the forgiveness of your sins. Then you will receive the gift of the Holy Spirit. 39 This promise is to you, to your children, and to those far away — all who have been called by the Lord our God."

Here is the crux of this message. The job of the Holy Spirit is to open the door for you to share Jesus. The reason God heals…open a life to Jesus. He confirms the future…to open a heart to receive Jesus. We have been doing it backward. We've been trying to get people saved…that is the job of the Holy Spirit. We've kept Him locked up in the back room, afraid He might disrupt our service, or He may go over the lunch hour. We have treated the Holy Spirit like the crazy uncle that lives with you. When company comes over, you give him a plate of food and a couple of Benadryl and put him in his bedroom, hoping he doesn't get all crazy and disrupt your dinner party.

Then notice in verse 38, he doesn't say "repent, turn to God, be baptized and you got everything you'll get." NO! He says to do these things, and then you will receive the gift of the Holy Spirit. He showed up in a whirlwind, and suddenly, **they were all speaking a language they had never spoken before.**

CHAPTER FIFTEEN

May I tell you that Bethel is no longer a geographical location. Bethel is around us all the time. If you haven't figured it out yet...let me help you. Bethel is not a specific location on Google Maps. Bethel is where the presence of God is. If you have received the gift of the Holy Spirit, Bethel is wherever you are!

We have been given the keys to this stairway, and we are afraid to turn the key. We can enter this divine sanctuary on a daily basis, and it is time for the church, the Body of Christ to step up and take our place as the gatekeepers of this heavenly realm. Please stay with me, because now that you know that God still speaks to us and we can talk to Him, then the most important step has been taken. When you realize that there is a stairway, then if you know your rightful place in this Kingdom, then you must realize that you have the right to use that stairway...the entrance into the Presence of Jehovah.

I know, some of you are thinking that this was the Old Testament and that this is "not for us today". I love people who search the scriptures daily and try to figure out why nothing applies to them. They love to find all the "here's why you can't have this." I want to look for all the reasons why I can have this or that.

Look at John 1:43-51… ". (Now from this point on, Jesus is speaking by the Spirit…a foretaste of the "word of knowledge")

Vs. 47 says *"As they approached, Jesus said, now here is a genuine son of Israel-a man of complete integrity." "How do you know about me?" Nathanael asked. Jesus replied, I could see you under the fig tree before Philip found you."* Then Nathanael exclaimed *"Rabbi, you are the Son of God-the king of Israel"*.

Let me stop here momentarily. This is a major key point for us. When you have a word of knowledge or a miracle takes place, the main purpose is to open the door for Jesus to be glorified, magnified and to be shown as the "Son of God"….not, "you are a miracle worker or you are a prophet". If you are getting the glory, then Jesus isn't, and that is the reason miracles happen. Ok? You are just the garden hose that is spraying the water…you're not the WATER!

Keep reading in vs. 50 *"Jesus asked him, 'Do you believe this just because I told you I had seen you under the fig tree? You will see great things than this.' Then I said…(hold on, here it comes) 'I tell you the truth, you will all see heaven open and the angels of God going up and down ON the Son of Man or the* **one who** *is the stairway between heaven and earth."*

Sorry, did you catch that? Jesus is referencing Genesis 28, where Jacob has a vision of the stairway into Heaven, and Jesus just says that yes, you are going to see angels of God going up and down on ME…you know… I AM THE STAIRWAY BETWEEN HEAVEN AND EARTH. In other words, it used to be impossible for a man to enter the heavenly arena…but not anymore. I AM THE STAIRWAY. You now have unfettered access into the very presence of God.

The key is knowing you already have the key to the stairway…His name is Jesus.

"You are just the garden hose that is spraying the water...you're not the WATER!"

CHAPTER SIXTEEN

Ok…let's get this down. Number one: God still speaks to us.

I need to address something. There are some who are calling the church board right now, telling them to be careful of this Dr. Weird guy because he is saying that God speaks to us today when we know He only speaks to us through His word, The Bible.

There are two Greek words for "word". The first word is Logos or the written word of God. Let me show you two examples of Logos:

1. *"For the word [logos] of God is living, and powerful"* (Hebrews 4:12).

2. *"Study to present yourself approved to God, a workman who does not to be*

ashamed, rightly dividing the word [logos] of truth" (II Timothy 2:15).

Listen, the Word of God is so powerful. It is God speaking through the ages, and the holy men of God wrote it down as they were inspired by the Holy Spirit. But there is another word for word…Rhema. Rhema is the spoken word of God. Let me show you:

1. *"If you abide in Me, and My words [rhema] abide in you, you will ask what you desire, and it shall be done unto you"* (John 15:7). Do you see this? God literally speaks a word…rhema…and with that you can ask and it shall be done. How? Your faith is primed and ready. How?

2. *"So then faith comes by hearing, and hearing by the word [rhema] of God"* (Romans 10:17). Do you see this? When you speak a word over someone who is so devastated and worn down by sickness or a situation of some kind, and suddenly they hear the word of the Lord and LIFE springs forth…faith increases, and they have the gas they need to get to the other side!

3. *"The words [rhema] that I speak to you are spirit, and they are life"* (John 6:63).

You see, what you are going to hear from Jesus is that He has come to bring life into all the dead dreams and visions of your life. Satan has come to kill, steal and destroy. So, if you hear someone say anything other than life…It is not the Holy Spirit.

Secondly, there is a staircase into this heavenly arena, and you have the key to the Kingdom of

God. You have the key to the storehouse of all possibilities. Someone is getting excited. Wait…there is more.

CHAPTER SEVENTEEN

So, we know that God still speaks to us and that there is a stairway to the heavens...the question is, what keeps us from entering this stairway area? We have to go back to Genesis chapter 3. Here is the picture: God creates man and woman and puts them into the garden. They have everything that they could ever want or need. Notice, they evidently don't need clothes. They were bebopping around the old garden in their birthday suits. Free as a bird. Until one day, there is a serpent in the garden, and he tells them (that is an entirely different topic of why a talking snake didn't catch them off guard!) that it is ok for them to eat this forbidden fruit. The snake was telling her that God wasn't talking literally...it was figuratively. Does that sound familiar? So, they ate this fruit. And at that moment, or IMMEDIATELY their eyes were opened, and they suddenly felt shame at their nakedness.

Let's clear something up. To the believer, someone who has confessed Jesus as the Lord of their life, sin does not keep you from heaven. Here is the amazing and refreshing promise of the Word. When Jesus was hanging on the cross, He was doing away with past, present and future and his blood washed away all sin. He washed away the very first sin of Adam and Eve.

Let me stop here a minute. Through the years, I have people tell me that they are so concerned that they have committed the "Unpardonable Sin". They just know they have. When I ask them, they tell of how they told a friend that they don't believe that Jesus heals any longer. In fact, their friend asked for prayer, and they prayed, but they just don't believe that He would forgive them. May I share something with you? You need to look at Matthew 26…it is going to change your life. We are talking about Peter…you know…the disciple of Jesus. They guy who said He was Gods gift to Jesus. He would stick with Him to the very end. Matthew 26: 69 *"Now Peter was sitting outside in the courtyard. And a servant girl came up to him and said, "You also were with Jesus the Galilean. 70 But he denied it before them all, saying, "I do not know what you are talking about. 71 And when he went out to the entrance, another servant girl saw him, and she said to the bystanders, "This man was with Jesus of Nazareth. 72 And again he denied it with an oath: "I do not know the man." 73 After a little while the bystanders came up and said to Peter, "Certainly you too are one of them, for your accent betrays you." 74 Then he began to invoke a curse on himself and to swear, "I do not know the man." And immediately the rooster crowed. 75 And Peter remembered the saying of Jesus, "Before the rooster crows, you will deny me three times." And he went out and wept bitterly"*

Do you understand this? Peter didn't just read about this Jesus 2000 years later…he was right there. He had seen all the miracles. He ate every meal with Him. He watched him heal people, when doctors had given up. He saw Him feed 5000 plus people with his own eyes. In fact, he helped pick up the left-overs. All of this, and yet as he is standing there in front of Him and when they asked Peter… "Do you know this guy"? He says "NO!" Now, one denial…I could get…maybe even the second. But the third time…not only does he say He doesn't know it, but he starts cussing like a drunken sailor. Do you think he wrestled with this? Oh yeah. It sounds to me that if anybody had committed that unpardonable sin, it was right here with Peter. But look at this… Matthew 16:18 *"Now I say to you that you are Peter (which means 'rock'), and upon this rock I will build my church, and all the powers of hell will not conquer it."* Not only did Jesus look beyond his sin, but He decides to build the church on the character of Peter. Do you know what else? On that cross, the shed blood of Jesus was spilled for all of humanity and on that cross…Peter's transgressions were completely wiped clean. Forgotten. So, He also looked down through eternity and not only forgave you the sins you committed when you were a little child, but he has already completely erased and eradicated the sin you might commit on your deathbed. You know what I am talking about! As you take your last breath and look at the beautiful nurse that walks in and you say "Dang..she is HOT"…wheeze…cough…you're gone. There are no sins present when you apply the finished work of Christ on the Cross of Calvary. Zilch…nada…disappeared forever.

But what sin does to you is to put you in the precarious position of shame. The enemy somehow convinces you that now you have so disappointed God that He could never hear you or speak to you again. You hide in the garden, too ashamed to spend time in His presence. Suddenly, you stop talking to God. You quite trying to hear His voice because you are so terrible. Ahhhhhh…remember the cross? Already forgiven. The plan part B handled that sin stuff. God just wants you to move into The Plan, Part C… the Church kicking some Devil Butt taking names and restoring the Kingdom.

Unlike Adam and Eve, they were living before The Plan, Part A was complete, Jesus had not died on the cross. Their mess does not apply to you. As a believer, you are covered by Romans chapter 8…read this…

Romans 8:31 *"What shall we say about such wonderful things as these? If God is for us, who can ever be against us? 32. Since he did not spare even his own Son but gave him up for us all, won't he also give us everything else? 33 Who dares accuse us whom God has chosen for his own? No one – for God himself has given us right standing with himself. 34 Who then will condemn us? No one – for Christ Jesus died for us and was raised to life for us, and he is sitting in the place of honor at God's right hand, pleading for us.*

35 Can anything ever separate us from Christ's love? Does it mean he no longer loves us if we have trouble or calamity, or are persecuted, or hungry, or destitute, or in danger, or threatened with death? 36 (As the Scriptures say, "For your sake we are killed every day; we are being slaughtered like sheep."[a]) 37 No, despite all these things, overwhelming victory is ours through Christ, who loved us.

38 And I am convinced that nothing can ever separate us from God's love. Neither death nor life, neither angels nor demons, neither our fears for today nor our worries about tomorrow – not even the powers of hell can separate us from God's love. 39 No power in the sky above or in the earth below – indeed, nothing in all creation will ever be able to separate us from the love of God that is revealed in Christ Jesus our Lord."

The only thing that can separate you from God now Is a lie you were told by the devil. His time is short, and he is trying to keep you from the staircase! I want to give you three keys to opening the door to the staircase....

On that cross, the shed blood of Jesus was spilled for all of humanity and on that cross…Peter's transgressions and your transgressions were completely wiped clean. Forgotten.

CHAPTER EIGHTEEN
THE FIRST KEY...WORSHIP

We know God still speaks. There is a staircase into the presence of Jehovah. He has work for you to do. He has gifts and a calling on your life. The question you should be asking right now is... "How can I hear God clearer, open the staircase, and walk in what He has called me to do? Why does God show up sometimes and not others?

First of all, it is our job to create an atmosphere where the presence of God is free to move and abide. It is an atmosphere where the Spirit of the Lord begins to stir, and answers come, diseases flee, and the future is clarified.

Go with me to an incredible meeting in the scriptures found in 2 Kings chapter 3. Remember Elijah is taken up into heaven and his cloak and anointing pass on to Elisha. This dude had been hanging out with Elijah and for him it was his school of the prophets. He learned from watching and the experiences how the Spirit of the Lord worked. He had seen firsthand the power of the anointing, and when Elijah was ready to leave, he asked Elisha, "What do you want?". For Elisha it was simple. Whatever you had, I'll have a double. Imagine the power that

was transferred to him. So now, Elisha is the prophet of the land of Israel. He is God's man for the hour. So when the nation of Israel came to a point of war, the King was looking for wisdom from God. Let's pick up with 2 Kings 3:
10 "What should we do?" the king of Israel cried out. "The LORD has brought the three of us here to let the king of Moab defeat us."

11 But King Jehoshaphat of Judah asked, "Is there no prophet of the LORD with us? If there is, we can ask the LORD what to do through him."

This king may have forgotten a lot, but he knew that the Holy Spirit was able to speak through men. He knew that if he could find a prophet of the Lord, he could find his answer. God is still looking for prophets to stand up and speak "Thus saith the Lord" to Governors, Kings, Presidents and CEO's!
"One of King Joram's officers replied, "Elisha, son of Shaphat, is here. He used to be Elijah's personal assistant."

12 "Jehoshaphat said, 'Yes, the LORD speaks through him.' So, the king of Israel, King Jehoshaphat of Judah, and the king of Edom went to consult with Elisha.

13 "Why are you coming to me?" Elisha asked the king of Israel. "Go to the pagan prophets of your father and mother!" In other words, for years you have turned your back on Jehovah...why are you wanting Him to help you now? Why can't your pagan Gods help you now? THEY CAN'T

But King Joram of Israel said, "No! For it was the LORD who called us three kings here—only to be defeated by the king of Moab!"
Elisha knew that they had forgotten the Lord their God. They had relied on false gods and images for answers, but none of that would help them now. They realized that they needed a word from the Lord.

The question we are asking in this chapter is how we get to the presence of God. How do we open up the "staircase" into the arena where everything is possible?

14 *"Elisha replied, "As surely as the LORD Almighty lives, whom I serve, I wouldn't even bother with you except for my respect for King Jehoshaphat of Judah. 15Now bring me someone who can play the harp. While the harp was being played, the power of the LORD came upon Elisha."*

He found an answer. He was close to finding the first key. He knew that the music was a key to opening up the portal to the presence of God. There is an incredible power in worship. It breaks strongholds and opens up the river of

God. When all of the pieces come together in worship, God moves.

As I have watched video after video of the great men and women of God who knew how to attract the presence of God in a service. They all knew the power of the worship that preceded their ministry time.

CHAPTER NINETEEN

2 Chronicles 20 tells us the story of Israel when they are again surrounded by enemies. Jehoshaphat is the King and he "remembers" and cries out. It begins in verse 13, *"As all the men of Judah stood before the LORD with their little ones, wives, and children, 14 the Spirit of the LORD came upon one of the men standing there. His name was Jahaziel son of Zechariah, son of Benaiah, son of Jeiel, son of Mattaniah, a Levite who was a descendant of Asaph.*

15 He said, "Listen, all you people of Judah and Jerusalem! Listen, King Jehoshaphat! This is what the LORD says: Do not be afraid! Don't be discouraged by this mighty army, for the battle is not yours, but God's."

A little-known man who hears the voice of the Lord has the audacity to stand up and proclaim to the KING…do not be afraid. I am talking to someone right now. You have been tormented by fear. You look in front, behind, above, below, and on each side of you, and all you see is defeat. But you aren't looking far enough. You need a word from the Lord.

16 "Tomorrow, march out against them. You will find them coming up through the ascent of Ziz at the end of the valley that opens into the wilderness of Jeruel.

17 But you will not even need to fight. Take your positions; then stand still and watch the LORD's victory. He is with you, O people of Judah and Jerusalem. Do not be afraid or discouraged. Go out against them tomorrow, for the LORD is with you!

18 Then King Jehoshaphat bowed low with his face to the ground. And all the people of Judah and Jerusalem did the same, worshiping the LORD.

The key to His presence is worship. It opens up the Bethel that is needed there at that time.

19 Then, the Levites from the clans of Kohath and Korah stood to praise the LORD, the God of Israel, with a very loud shout."

We have a church now that is so afraid that we are going to embarrass the unbelievers and scare them away when we get loud in our worship. When we lift our hands or God forbid, start to sing in the Spirit in a service. These folks in verse 19 were not ashamed, nor were they quiet.

20 "Early the next morning, the army of Judah went out into the wilderness of Tekoa. On the way, Jehoshaphat stopped and said, "Listen to me, all you people of Judah and Jerusalem! Believe in the LORD your God, and you will be able to stand firm. Believe in his prophets, and you will succeed."

21 After consulting the people, the king appointed singers to walk ahead of the army, singing to the LORD and praising him for his holy splendor."

Did you see that? He didn't put the heavy-duty tanks or the B52 Bombers out first. He wanted to hit them hard...Shock and Awe so He put the Worshippers FIRST. He realized that they would open up the portal for the Lord God almighty to show up and HE could fight the battle.

"This is what they sang:

"Give thanks to the LORD;

his faithful love endures forever!"

22 At the very moment they began to sing and give praise, the LORD caused the armies of Ammon, Moab, and Mount Seir to start fighting among themselves."

You have been trying to fight the enemy on your own. You see, when you worship and praise, the devil doesn't have a chance. Suddenly, all of his imps, the very demonic forces that have been assigned to cause your demise start to fight among themselves. **If you do this the right way...you DO NOT EVEN HAVE TO FIGHT!** Let me talk to Pastor for a second. I think that if you look over all of your services, the time when you got up to preach and the Word flowed like warm honey out of your mouth and lives were changed…were times when praise and worship was on fire. Look back at those services…it was those services when miracles happened. Don't be too quick to jump into your message…make sure God is ready for you to move on. You may find a service every once and a while, that you can't stand up and preach that sermon you worked for 30 hours on…God may have another plan!

23 *"The armies of Moab and Ammon turned against their allies from Mount Seir and killed every one of them. After they had destroyed the army of Seir, they began attacking each other. 24 So when the army of Judah arrived at the lookout point in the wilderness, all they saw were dead bodies lying on the ground as far as they could see. Not a single one of the enemy had escaped.*

25 King Jehoshaphat and his men went out to gather the plunder. They found vast amounts of equipment, clothing, and other valuables – more than they could carry. There was so much plunder that it took them three days just to collect it all! 26 On the fourth day, they gathered in the Valley of Blessing, which got its name that day because the people praised and thanked the LORD there. It is still called the Valley of Blessing today."

You have been trying to fight the enemy on your own. You see, when you worship and praise, the devil doesn't have a chance. Suddenly, all of his imps, the very demonic forces that have been assigned to cause your demise start to fight among themselves. If you do this the right way…you **DO NOT EVEN HAVE TO FIGHT!**

CHAPTER TWENTY

Look through the Word. King David knew that he had the ability to create the atmosphere of Glory with worship. He wrote so many songs of praise and worship. Read the Psalms again. Most of them were just the Holy Spirit talking about this Jesus who was going to come and save them. He knew about Bethel and the stairs.

One of my favorite stories in the Bible is when King David recaptures the Ark of the Covenant. You see, it had been stolen by the enemy. David knew that this was a key to the success of Israel. He puts aside everything and goes and takes it back. Let's pick up with 2 Samuel 6

6 "Then David again gathered all the elite troops in Israel, 30,000 in all. 2 He led them to Baalah of Judah to bring back the Ark of God, which bears the name of the Lord of Heaven's Armies, who is enthroned between the cherubim. 3 They placed the Ark of God on a new cart and brought it from Abinadab's house, which was on a hill. Uzzah and Ahio, Abinadab's sons, were guiding the cart 4 that carried the Ark of God. Ahio walked in front of the Ark. 5 David and all the people of Israel were celebrating before the Lord, singing songs and playing all kinds of musical instruments – lyres, harps, tambourines, castanets, and cymbals.

6 But when they arrived at the threshing floor of Nacon, the oxen stumbled, and Uzzah reached out his hand and steadied the Ark of God. 7 Then the Lord's anger was aroused against Uzzah, and God struck him dead because of this. So Uzzah died right there beside the Ark of God."

This is an entire book unto itself…maybe for later. The part of this scripture that I want you to see is found below. Keep reading this.

8 "David was angry because the Lord's anger had burst out against Uzzah. He named that place Perez-uzzah (which means "to burst out against Uzzah"), as it is still called today.

9 David was now afraid of the Lord, and he asked, "How can I ever bring the Ark of the Lord back into my care?" 10 So David decided not to move the Ark of the Lord into the City of David. **Instead, he took it to the house of Obed-edom of Gath. 11 The Ark of the Lord remained there in Obed-edom's house for three months, and the Lord blessed Obed-edom and his entire household.***"*

I want you to just imagine this. David captures back the Ark, but someone messed up and touched the ark. The new translation, that I am just writing says, "And David got freaked out.". So, he finds a man, Obed-Edom and asks him to put it in his HOUSE. This may have been a point of contention with his wife, but he takes out the dining room table and in it's place, the Ark of God goes there. (No, not Noahs ark, the Ark of the Covenant.) So, he wakes up every morning, and in his house is the Ark of the Covenant…you know where the presence of God abides. How different would your life be if that Ark was in your dining room? It did make a HUGE difference… Guess what? He is already there! Act like it!

12 Then King David was told, "The Lord has blessed Obed-edom's household and everything he has because of the Ark of God." So David went there and brought the Ark of God from the house of Obed-edom to the City of David with a great celebration. 13 After the men who were carrying the Ark of the Lord had gone six steps, David sacrificed a bull and a fattened calf. 14 And David danced before the Lord with all his might, wearing a priestly garment. 15 So David and all the people of Israel brought up the Ark of the Lord with shouts of joy and the blowing of rams' horns."

Obed-edom has spent 6 months of his life with the Ark of God in his house. It changed his life forever. Do you think he was a little disappointed when David comes back to move the Ark to the special tabernacle? Sure! But his involvement doesn't stop here. Move over to 1 Chronicles chapter 15 and pick up with verse 16 *"David also ordered the Levite leaders to appoint a choir of Levites who were singers and musicians to sing joyful songs to the accompaniment of harps, lyres, and cymbals. 17 So the Levites appointed Heman son of Joel along with his fellow Levites: Asaph son of Berekiah, and Ethan son of Kushaiah from the clan of Merari. 18 The following men were chosen as their assistants: Zechariah, Jaaziel,[b] Shemiramoth, Jehiel, Unni, Eliab, Benaiah, Maaseiah, Mattithiah, Eliphelehu, Mikneiah, and the* **gatekeepers — Obed-edom and Jeiel.**

19 The musicians Heman, Asaph, and Ethan were chosen to sound the bronze cymbals. 20 Zechariah, Aziel, Shemiramoth, Jehiel, Unni, Eliab, Maaseiah, and Benaiah were chosen to play the harps. 21 Mattithiah, Eliphelehu, Mikneiah, **Obed-edom***, Jeiel, and Azaziah were chosen to play the lyres. 22 Kenaniah, the head Levite, was chosen as the choir leader because of his skill.*

23 Berekiah and Elkanah were chosen to guard[e] the Ark. 24 Shebaniah, Joshaphat, Nethanel, Amasai, Zechariah, Benaiah, and Eliezer — all of whom were priests — were chosen to blow the trumpets as they marched in front of the Ark of God. **Obed-edom and Jehiah were chosen to guard the Ark".**

This dude won't let go. Would you? He had the Ark of the Covenant in his house. Imagine trying to watch some skanky movie on your television in the living room with the Ark of the

Covenant in your dining room. You couldn't. But more important, it was the presence of God that changed him. The fact is, under the finished work of Christ, the presence of God is no longer in an Ark…it's in YOU!

So now we find out 2 things about Obed-Edom. 1. He is a musician. He has seen God move when worship takes place. He knew the relationship between music and God's presence. Number 2, is that David set him in as one of two people responsible to guard the Ark. Do you think that this guy would stand aside and let another enemy steal the Ark? No way. He knew that their future…depended on the presence of God in their midst. David knew he would guard it with all of his life.

But that is not the end.

One of my favorite scriptures is Psalm 84. I realize it is a little bit long, but I think you need to read the entire chapter.

1 "How lovely is your dwelling place,
  O Lord of Heaven's Armies.
2 I long, yes, I faint with longing
  to enter the courts of the Lord.
With my whole being, body and soul,
  I will shout joyfully to the living God.
3 Even the sparrow finds a home,

*and the swallow builds her nest and raises her young
at a place near your altar,
    O Lord of Heaven's Armies, my King and my God!
4 What joy for those who can live in your house,
    always singing your praises. Interlude*

*5 What joy for those whose strength comes from the Lord,
    who have set their minds on a pilgrimage to Jerusalem.
6 When they walk through the Valley of Weeping,[b]
    it will become a place of refreshing springs.
    The autumn rains will clothe it with blessings.
7 They will continue to grow stronger,
    and each of them will appear before God in Jerusalem.[c]*

*8 O Lord God of Heaven's Armies, hear my prayer.
    Listen, O God of Jacob. Interlude*

*9 O God, look with favor upon the king, our shield!
    Show favor to the one you have anointed.*

**10 A single day in your courts
    is better than a thousand anywhere else!
I would rather be a gatekeeper in the house of my God
    than live the good life in the homes of the wicked.**
11 For the Lord God is our sun and our shield.

> *He gives us grace and glory.*
> *The Lord will withhold no good thing*
>   *from those who do what is right.*
> *12 O Lord of Heaven's Armies,*
>   *what joy for those who trust in you."*

Psalm 84, as with many of the Psalms, was not written by David. It is attributed to one of the Sons of Korah. According to Easton's Bible Dictionary, it was a Servant of Edom. (1.) "The Gittite" (probably so called because he was a native of Gath-rimmon), a Levite of the family of the Korhites (1 Chronicles 26:1, 4-8), to whom was specially intrusted the custody of the ark (1 Chronicles 15:18). Do you see this? Who wrote this chapter? Obededom. **The guy who had God's presence in his house for 6 months and now would gladly be a gatekeeper, just to be in His presence. And now you know... the rest of the story.**

Obededom knew how to gain this access into the presence of God. He knew that worship in music draws the Presence of God.

We have so much music in the church today. We have songs that have been written, and we love them, but they don't open up the stairway. If you knew how many songs that we sing in "worship" that have been written under the influence of drugs or alcohol, but not the anointing of the Holy Spirit, you would faint. They make for a great service, but I want the Heavens to open, and we create an atmosphere where the glory of God resides, people are healed, saved and filled with this Holy Spirit. Believe it or not, even the music soaks up the anointing. There are some songs that have been sung for 30 years, that when you sing them, you can feel the presence of God move into a room and suddenly, everything becomes possible.

I would rather be a gatekeeper in the house of my God than live the good life in the homes of the wicked.

CHAPTER TWENTY ONE

We are looking for the keys that open up the portal into the heavenly realm. **Worship is key number one.**

The **second key** is powerful, but to many controversial. I already slipped it in earlier but didn't push it too hard. Now is the time to push. For us in this time, it started on the day of Pentecost, when they were all together, in unity at a Bethel point. Suddenly, the heavens opened, and a mighty rushing wind blew in, carrying the presence of God in the form of the Holy Spirit. You see, these folks had seen manifestations of Him earlier but never to this amount. They saw prophets of God who were filled with this incredible power, but not Jerry who worked at the Jerusalem Walmart. Suddenly, every believer has the ability to be filled to overflowing with the power of the Holy Spirit.

The second key is the gift of praying in the Spirit or praying in tongues. Read what Paul says to the church in I Corinthians 14:1-2 *"Let love be your highest goal! But you should also desire the special abilities the Spirit gives – especially the ability to prophesy.*

2 For if you have the ability to speak in tongues, you will be talking only to God since people won't be able to understand you. You will be speaking by the power of the Spirit, but it will all be mysterious."

It is awesome. He is admonishing us to DESIRE the special abilities the Spirit gives. Here is where the controversy begins. The distinguishing between the "praying in tongues and the gift of tongues in a service." This incredible gift gives you the ability to speak to God…not people….to God. He then says, "You will be speaking by the power of the Spirit, but it will all be Mysterious". My Lord…do you see what we have been missing? We have been talked out of this crazy thing called "praying in the Spirit". To those who don't believe, they say it is just jibberish. Nonsensical talk.

Paul helps us to understand this in Romans chapter 8. Look at what he says starting in verse 26 *"And the Holy Spirit helps us in our weakness. For example, we don't know what God wants us to pray for. But the Holy Spirit prays for us with groanings that cannot be expressed in words. 27 And the Father who knows all hearts knows what the Spirit is saying, for the Spirit pleads for us believers in harmony with God's own will. 28 And we know that God causes everything to work together for the good of those who love God and are called according to his purpose for them."*
Want to know God's purpose for your life? Pray in the Spirit.

Do you see this? How many times have you heard someone say, "Pray for me; I'm having surgery." Ok. But what do I pray? "Lord, please guide the surgeon's hand so that the incision goes up 23 millimeters and then deep through the epithelial tissue into the surface muscles and not so deep so as to cut the intestines." Really? I don't know what to pray, but the Spirit does.

Go back to I Cor 14:14, "For if I pray in tongues, my spirit is praying, but I don't understand what I am saying.

That's ok. It is not you praying. It is your spirit praying. Instead of human flesh speaking to spirit…it is now spirit speaking directly to Spirit. You see, it is not words you are speaking, you are groaning with words that just can't be uttered. You are speaking mysteries. As you pray in the spirit, suddenly you are speaking out things that are not "thinking about saying". When you speak to someone, you have to literally sit there and think about what you are forming the words in your mind so that they come out in the right order and use the right words. Not when you pray in the spirit. Your spirit is praying.
When you are "praying in the Spirit or in tongues",

do you think God is listening to the "words" you are saying? Can you imagine God is talking to one of the angels and suddenly you start to pray in the spirit. He stops talking to the angels…. "hold on…Tim is praying in tongues. Someone get me the dictionary. Michael…did he just say 'shumma bo kamabulache or kamalacheche? QUIET…everyone I need to hear exactly what Tim is saying." NO! You are praying spirit to Spirit. For those who poopoo this and make fun of you, saying you are speaking things nobody understands….BAM. That's just what Paul said….you are speaking mysteries.

Now look at verse 15 *"Well then, what shall I do? I will pray in the spirit, and I will also pray in words I understand. I will sing in the spirit, and I will also sing in words I understand."*

Now suddenly, I am able to pray with my human mind…my understanding. I can pray for what I do know in the natural…but now I can also pray in the spirit-to-Spirit connection. For every nuance of this situation, I do not know anything about…the Spirit does, and He communicates that with my spirit. Then look at "I will sing in the spirit". Now he fuses the power of the key of worship with the power of the unknown tongues in worship. I can sing in the spirit. I just intensified my worship by 1000X. We need to be careful so as not to let this get too crazy because that will repel guests. Oh Hell no! These people are hurting and searching for someone who can tap into the power of Bethel. They are looking for a place that understands that can help them be a world overcomer. They are looking for the Holy Spirit to lead them to Jesus!

I cannot tell you how many times I walk around my clinic and suddenly I begin to pray in the spirit. Don't know what about…but the Spirit does. I don't know what enemy was just thwarted or what person near me was ready to end it all. I don't know these things…but God does.

I want you to take another look at Ephesians 6…with new eyes!

10 "A final word: Be strong in the Lord and in his mighty power. 11 Put on all of God's armor so that you will be able to stand firm against all strategies of the devil. 12 For are not fighting against flesh-and-blood enemies, but against evil rulers and authorities of the unseen world, against mighty powers in this dark world, and against evil spirits in the heavenly places.

13Therefore, put on every piece of God's armor so you will be able to resist the enemy in the time of evil. Then after the battle you will still be standing firm. 14

Stand your ground, putting on the belt of truth and the body armor of God's righteousness. 15 For shoes, put on the peace that comes from the Good News so that you will be fully prepared. 16 In addition to all of these, hold up the shield of faith to stop the fiery arrows of the devil.17 Put on salvation as your helmet, and take the sword of the Spirit, which is the word of God.

18 Pray in the Spirit at all times and on every occasion. Stay alert and be persistent in your prayers for all believers everywhere."

Here is where we have fallen short. We see everything in the flesh. We have been taught to "believe in science" or that "math doesn't lie". We have been praying with those things in mind because we can taste them, feel them, smell them! Can I tell you that the reason we don't see our prayers answered more, is that we are in a gun fight, and we are throwing cotton balls in our underwear! Put on this iron clad armor and don't take cotton balls to a gun fight!

If I wake up in the middle of the night…I realize that "God gives His beloved rest" and so there must be a reason I am awake. Sometimes, I get a flash picture of someone, and I begin to pray in the spirit. I don't know what is going on or what they need, but the Holy Spirit does. If you wake up and look at the clock night after night and it is

3:33 or 2:22, I believe that God will do fun things to get your attention. For certain, you need to spend time praying. Remember, this is "spirit talk". You don't have to pray out loud all the time... you can pray in your mind....silently. So powerful! Put your armor on and lay there praying in the prayer language that God has given you!

Now let me hit this because there are some who are going to tell you that prophecy is more important than "tongues". Well certainly. You decide. What is more powerful? I go to the grocery store and find someone and start to speak in my prayer language out loud to them or if I am talking to someone at the grocery store, is it more powerful if I can tell them that on the way to work, they were almost in an accident, and God saved them and that He loves them? Stop letting people try to talk you out of your promises in the Word. I am tired of the impotent church telling me to quiet down and not get carried away with this kind of nonsense. If they tell you that, shake the dust off your shoes right in their marble foyer and "run, Forest, run". Find a church home where God is glorified, Jesus is Lord and the Holy Spirit is not locked in the Janitors closet. You want to be in a place of Bethel where there is a tornado with every service. **But I am here to tell you, you won't see**

the prophetic words until you have saturated yourself in your supernatural prayer language.

This is a package deal. You can't have one without the other!
1. Praying in the Spirit. The Holy Spirit is strategizing. He is preparing you…building up your faith so that…

2. Prophecy can happen.

May I tell you that the people who give the 1 minute powerful prophetic word from God have spent HOURS praying in the Holy Ghost. What are you waiting for?

Can I tell you that the reason we don't see our prayers answered more, is that we are in a gun fight, and we are sitting in our pajamas, throwing cotton balls! Put on this iron clad armour and don't take cotton balls to a gun fight!

CHAPTER TWENTY TWO

The next, but probably not the final key to opening up the portal to the presence of God is this…hearing the still, small voice…and then acting on it.

Remember Samuel? Here is a little boy who has been living near the presence of God in the Tabernacle. Remember…that God wasn't saying much in those days. That doesn't mean He didn't want to, but no one was listening. Here is old Eli…so decrepit and worn out…he wasn't listening. If he were, he would have known his boys were messing with God's anointing and creating havoc in the house of God. God used a little boy. Three times God spoke. Samuel knew it was God…Eli didn't. Not until the third time. Finally, Eli wakes up from his spiritual stupor and tells Samuel what to do.

I Samuel 3:10 *"And the LORD came and called as before, "Samuel! Samuel!"*

And Samuel replied, "Speak, your servant is listening."

11 Then the LORD said to Samuel, "I am about to do a shocking thing in Israel. 12 I am going to carry out all my threats against Eli and his family, from beginning to end. 13 I have warned him that judgment is coming upon his family forever, because his sons are blaspheming God and he hasn't disciplined them. 14 So I have vowed that the sins of Eli and his sons will never be forgiven by sacrifices or offerings."

15 Samuel stayed in bed until morning, then got up and opened the doors of the Tabernacle as usual. He was afraid to tell Eli what the LORD had said to him. 16 But Eli called out to him, "Samuel, my son."

"Here I am," Samuel replied.

17 "What did the LORD say to you? Tell me everything. And may God strike you and even kill you if you hide anything from me!" 18 So Samuel told Eli everything; he didn't hold anything back. "It is the LORD's will," Eli replied. "Let him do what he thinks best."

The fact is, Eli should have heard it BEFORE Samuel did! He was too distracted…too overwhelmed. Too tired of spending time in the presence of God.

There are times when God will use you, and you don't understand what in the world it means. It doesn't make sense or it isn't always a "feel good" message. Be ready to say, "Speak, Lord, for thy servant hears."

CHAPTER TWENTY THREE

Now here is where we often get knocked off the horse. We hear God speak. We listen to that still small voice and then the enemy comes in and tries to talk you out of what God has told you.

Don't worry; this has been going on for a long time. You're not the only one. Follow me back to the very beginning in the Garden of Eden. You know the story. In Genesis 2, God had created man and gave him dominion over every living thing: dogs, cats, flowers, and trees...everything but the special tree in the middle of the garden. This tree was the knowledge of good and evil. And he was quite specific...you eat it...you die.

So then we pick up with Genesis 3:1. *"The serpent was the shrewdest of all the wil animals the Lord God had made. One day he asked the woman, 'did God really say you must not eat the fruit from any of the trees in the garden?'*

Here is where we get knocked off....the devil will try to get you to doubt that you heard from God. Did He really say that to you or are you having that anxiety issue again? Are you just hearing the voices of people in the past talking to you? You see, the Devil is not that good. He has used the same tactics for thousands of years…**trying to get people to doubt God's word to them.**

He is STILL trying to talk you out of this call of God for your life. Let me give you some of the things that Satan will whisper in your ear….you ready?

"Oh…God has a doorway to open up to receive power so that you can touch the people around you????

1. You're too old

2. You're too young

3. You're too fat

4. You're too skinny

5. You have too much "baggage" from your life before Jesus.

6. Sure that person gave you a "word from the Lord", but he doesn't know what you have done.

I am I talking to you right now? If so, don't put this book down because God is going to set you free!

You see, for years, we have doubted the word of the Lord. We have felt like we need to "judge" every word spoken over us. We have felt that we need to wait to see if it comes to pass to make sure that this person was speaking the word of the Lord.

We have allowed the enemy to rob us of some amazing truths and direction in our life because we had to "test these prophetic words."

You see, the Devil is not that good. He has used the same tactics for thousands of years…**trying to get people to doubt God's word to them.**

There IS a test to the prophetic words spoken, but it is not what you think it is. The Holy Spirit led me to His written Logos word to back up His spoken Rhema word. Listen to what the author of I John 4 says in regard to discerning false prophets.

1 "Dear friends, do not believe everyone who claims to speak by the Spirit. You must test them to see if the spirit they have comes from God. For there are many false prophets in the world. 2 This is how we know if they have the Spirit of God: If a person claiming to be a prophet acknowledges that Jesus Christ came in a real body, that person has the Spirit of God. 3 But if someone claims to be a prophet and does not acknowledge the truth about Jesus, that person is not from God. Such a person has the spirit of the Antichrist, which you heard is coming into the world and indeed is already here."

You see, it is the acknowledgment that Jesus is the son of the living God; that is what shows that a prophet is from God

4 *"But you belong to God, my dear children. You have already won a victory over those people, because the Spirit who lives in you is greater than the spirit who lives in the world. 5 Those people belong to this world, so they speak from the world's viewpoint, and the world listens to them. 6 But we belong to God, and those who know God listen to us. If they do not belong to God, they do not listen to us. That is how we know if someone has the Spirit of truth or the spirit of deception."*

Imagine if the people had used the "wait to see if the prophecy comes to pass before we believe it test" had been used on Isaiah. In Isaiah 7:13-14, an exasperated Isaiah speaks to the people of God. Then Isaiah said, 13 *"Listen well, you royal family of David! Isn't it enough to exhaust human patience? Must you exhaust the patience of my God as well? 14 All right then, the Lord himself will give you the sign. Look! The virgin will conceive a child! She will give birth to a son and will call him Immanuel (which means 'God is with us')."*

Look at verse 14 above... You see, Isaiah had heard the voice of God enough to know that God had indeed spoken a word to him. He knew that what God had said, He would bring it to pass.

He didn't know that it would take thousands of years…and yet through the ages, the seasoned prophet had enough clout for millions of people through the millennia to believe the word that God had spoken through the ages.

It is the same today. There are times when God may speak to you to do this or that or say this…and it just doesn't make sense. You have heard that still, small voice enough to know that God is speaking and you need to share it.

> I will never forget getting ready to walk into an exam room with a brand-new patient. I had never met her, and she didn't know me from Adam. As I walked through the door, I felt that nudge and heard it in my spirit, "sing that song from the movie Frozen…Let is go". Now listen, so some they would say that is stupid. Disney is horrible…God wouldn't say that. That is just unprofessional in a doctor's office. But I wasn't listening to the serpent. I get my marching orders from someone greater. So, I walked through the door and started singing "Let it go…let it go" and she burst out crying. As she composed herself, she said that was her daughter's favorite song and today was the anniversary of her death 5 years ago. You see…God knew her and knew exactly what would get her attention so He could introduce her to Jesus….the healer of broken

> hearts. God did in 5 seconds what a therapist in 20 years of counseling could never do…he gave her a new heart.

Now, if you have never "given a word of knowledge" or a "prophetic word" …don't try it right out of the gate. Let God season you by giving you words, and you see them come to pass.

I was just new to this new world of the Spirit of God. I was in my little chiropractic practice/ weekend pastor gig. Every morning, I would walk from my house about 10 blocks to my office since we were just starting in life and only had one car. I had just prayed, "God I want you to use me. I want to learn how to hear your voice clearly and accurately." So on my way to the office one morning, I am walking and praying in tongues. I walk past a little house…nothing special…. just a house. As I walked past it, I heard the Holy Spirit say "someone just now died in that house". I looked at the house and it was dark because I left for work early. I had already learned to pray in the Spirit as much as I could. I remember thinking…hmmmm….no ambulances or hearses… I could have doubted that word from God, but I CHOSE to believe the Lord. Well, 3 days later, I come home from work and there is a hearse there with several cars. It happens every once and a while that someone has their funeral in their home and not at the funeral home. They probably didn't know why they chose to have their funeral at home, but I do. God was teaching me to hear his voice. Start to turn on the sensitivity to hearing God speak.

Part of the reason that we don't hear the "still, small voice of the Holy Spirit", is that we are so distracted. We are watching so much TV that it blows my mind. We know all the words from the latest Beyonce song, but can't recite a single Bible verse. We know all of the scores from every football player of every team since 1901, and we can't memorize one single Bible verse. Oooopsss, I am stepping on toes now. Want some other toes stepped on? We have headphones on our heads for 22 hours a day, and you know what....you can be listening to your favorite worship singers....but you are distracted. I love music. I love great worship songs. This was about the time where you would buy some tv evangelists cassette tapes and listen to them every waking moment. I love to hear some good preaching, but if I listen to that all the time, I don't have time to hear the voice of God. Remember, faith comes from the Rhema Word of God. Do you understand what I am saying? Even Jesus had to "get away" to pray. Some place where the tv isn't blaring, or the internet isn't taking your attention with TikTok or Facebook. You need to hear God now more than ever.

You see, the Devil is not that good. He has used the same tactics for thousands of years…trying to get people to doubt God's word to them. Why should he change? It is still working for him!

CHAPTER TWENTY FOUR

Let's recap. The keys to this staircase are simple:
1. Worship. Learn to love being in the presence of God. Learn how to create the atmosphere where God abides.

2. Pray in the Spirit. Every chance you get, use your supernatural Holy Ghost Prayer language.

3. Learn to trust that still, small voice of the Holy Spirit. He will speak to you anytime you are willing to listen.

Finally, let me say this. We have mistakenly thought God wants to give me these incredible gifts so that I can stand up in church and give these "words" of Wisdom, Knowledge, Prophecy and healing for the people in the church. Not so much. I really believe that everything in the service needs to be done decently and in order. And yet, there needs to be the willingness to have a service where the Holy Spirit is given free reign, and He can move however He sees fit. There are so many times when I could literally speak a word to a congregation….but that is not my congregation. There is a shepherd over that flock and I am part of that flock. Now, I have also been in the service where the pastor invited me to share words of knowledge and healing in a service. I believe the pastors' main job is to teach the people how to minister. His main job is to prepare you for ministry in your world…your sphere of influence. Look at Ephesians 4… 11 *"Now these are the gifts Christ gave to the church: the apostles, the prophets, the evangelists, and the pastors and teachers. 12 Their responsibility is to equip God's people to do his work and build up the church, the body of Christ. 13 This will continue until we all come to such unity in our faith and knowledge of God's Son that we will be mature in the Lord, measuring up to the full and complete standard of Christ."*

It is his job to help you grow in your gifts. You know all the spiritual gifts that guide people to Jesus. "Well, Dr. Tim Weir, if we aren't going to use them in the church service, where are we going to use them?" Believe me, I have known several people who have left churches because the pastor would let them belt out a message in tongues or prophecy. Let me show you this great nugget. Moses is getting ready to put together the big Tabernacle and God is giving him directions on how to build this. Look with me at Exodus 31:1-4 *" Then the LORD said to Moses, 2 "Look, I have specifically chosen Bezalel son of Uri, grandson of Hur, of the tribe of Judah. 3I have filled him with the Spirit of God, giving him great wisdom, ability, and expertise in all kinds of crafts. 4*

He is a master craftsman, expert in working with gold, silver, and bronze. 5He is skilled in engraving and mounting gemstones and in carving wood."

He is a master at his craft!

Did you see verse 2? I picked out a son of Uri from the tribe of Judah…PRAISE. He filled him with the Spirit of God, giving him Wisdom, ability and expertise in all kinds of crafts. He had a career…he was a craftsman. He had mastered his craft. God called him IN his craft to grow the Kingdom.

For years, I struggled with being in the ministry. I felt as if God had given me all these gifts…music….healing the sick… and prophetic-type gifts…He must want me in the full-time ministry. I believe a couple of pastors I sat under were institutionalized from hearing me talk about this all the time. Then I realized that God had called me and trained me for what I was doing. I realized that when I became the best of the best at what I do, it would attract thousands of patients and people who needed my skill, and it gave me the platform for allowing the Holy Spirit to move through me and my practice. I really believe God has enough preachers. I love preachers. But there are some who were called and some who just went! God has enough preachers…but he needs more Spirit-filled plumbers, physicians, teachers, lawyers, trash collectors, street-sweepers, Walmart clerks, businesswomen, etc. He is looking for these secret agents who will sharpen their craft, learn how to hear His voice and speak Jesus into the lives of people. He wants you to be the best of the best at what you are doing right now. He wants you to excel where He has you right now before He can trust you elsewhere. Don't be so distracted by "wanting to be in the ministry that you do your job half-a**ed!

Please don't try to be so spiritual that while you are at your computer doing your job…you read your Bible. That is stealing from your company. You are being paid to do a job…do it to the best of your ability. People are watching you. That is your testimony to the people who are watching you. Sometimes He just may want you to simply listen to someone who needs someone to hear them. But often, He want to use you to speak life and healing and restoration into a hurting, dying world.

We have let Satan pull us off target long enough. We have allowed the church to become a weak, pathetic, impotent fearful being, and God is looking for a remnant who will do what He asked us to do.

Here are your marching orders found in Mark 16

And then he told them, *15 "Go into all the world and preach the Good News to everyone. 16 Anyone who believes and is baptized will be saved. But anyone who refuses to believe will be condemned. 17 These miraculous signs will accompany those who believe: They will cast out demons in my name, and they will speak in new languages. 18 They will be able to handle snakes with safety, and if they drink anything poisonous, it won't hurt them. They will be able to place their hands on the sick, and they will be healed."*

19 When the Lord Jesus had finished talking with them, he was taken up into heaven and sat down in the place of honor at God's right hand. 20 And the disciples went everywhere and preached, and the Lord worked through them, confirming what they said by many miraculous signs."

Jesus finished the work. He had completed His task. He ripped the veil separating us from the Most Holy Place, giving you free access to the Father. He has completely defeated the enemy and now He has turned to you and given you the task of taking the message to your world. He has made available every gift and tool you need to complete it.

"Then you will receive the gift of the Holy Spirit. This promise is to you, to your children, and to those far away — all who have been called by the

Lord our God." The last part of that verse is YOU. He said this over 2000 years ago and He had you on His mind.

NOW IT IS UP TO YOU…THE DOORWAY WAS OPENED 2000 YEARS AGO. ALL YOU HAVE TO DO IS WALK INTO HIS PRESENCE! HE'S RIGHT THERE WITH YOU!

My prayer for you…

"Jesus, breath new life into my friend who is reading this book today. Fill them to overflowing so that out of their bellies flow rivers of living water, and they speak words they have never heard. The language of power….the language of the Spirit. I'm speaking to you right now…be baptized in the Holy Spirit in the name of Jesus Christ….the Son of the Living God…Be Filled."

RECEIVE THE GIFT OF THE HOLY SPIRIT!

Dr Tim Weir is a practicing chiropractor in Raleigh, NC. His post-graduate education in Trauma has helped him become an expert in car crash injuries. He has a mini-fellowship in MRI Interpretation and another one in Extremities from the SUNY Jacobs School of Medicine Buffalo. He is the first chiropractor in the United States to earn a Fellowship in Primary Spine care from the same Medical School.

Dr Weir took his work with Fibromyalgia patients and he is the author of the book, "Overcoming Fibromyalgia: A Practical Guide to Reclaiming Your Health". He is the formulator of Dr. Weir's Relax Formula for sleep issues.

Dr. Weir is the host of the popular "Loving Life with Dr. Weir" TV Show that is shown on the Your Home TV Network. This show, watched by over 1,000,000 people every month helps people navigate through life with hope and purpose.

Dr Tim Weir

5821 Falls of Neuse Rd Raleigh, NC 27609

If you would like Dr. Weir minister at your church, or you have a testimony to tell, email us at DrTimWeir@Gmail.com

www.FollowMeToTheStaircase.com

www.LakeCityChurch.org

www.DrMarkChironna.com

www.crossassembly.org

ALL SCRIPTURE REFERENCES ARE FROM THE NLT (New Living Translation)

Made in the USA
Middletown, DE
29 April 2024